D1739342

HARVESTMAN

HARVESTMAN

23 UNTITLED POEMS & COLLECTED LYRICS

STEVE VON TILL

Astrophil Press
at University of South Dakota
2020

The collected lyrics have previously appeared in the albums dated accordingly; *As the Crow Flies*, 1999; *If I Should Fall to the Field*, 2002; *A Grave is a Grim Horse*, 2008; *A Life Unto Itself,* 2015, *No Wilderness Deep Enough*, 2020.

Typesetting: Steve Von Till

Author's website: www.vontill.org

All linocut illustrations by Mazatl: www.graficamazatl.com

Astrophil Press at University of South Dakota
1st pressing 2020
Printed in the United States of America

Library of Congress Cataloging-in-Publication Data
Steve Von Till
Harvestman/Steve Von Till
        p. cm.
  ISBN 978-0-9980199-2-5 (pbk. : paper)
   1.Poetry, American   2. Music, American
Library of Congress Control Number: 9780998019925

http://www.astrophilpress.com

Dedicated to my shining ones.

Table of Contents

23 UNTITLED POEMS & COLLECTED LYRICS

2020

I

We have the sea
And we will always have the sky
There, in our own shadow
And in the absolute absence of stars
A darkness of depths
Illuminates who we are

II

Midnight migrations of mind
Toward pastures of delusion
Hanging halfway over the dark edge
Of that sheer and craggy cliff
That towers high above reason

With a skull full of stars
And a moon full of hearts
We weep the deadly river
And drift back to its source
The headwaters of ourselves

III

The millstone
Painted shades of moss and lichen
Stares blankly at the elder black ash
Longing to return to work

The river
Once deep red with the blood of toil
Laughs at the rotting boards of the water wheel
For they cannot slow her down

The bones
Bleached and removed of flesh
Lie scattered among the decaying leaves
Wanting only of spirit

The fog
Thickly veiled in its own mystery
Embraces it all with arms of vapour
Obscuring both death and life

IV

It is written on one's skin
That death often precedes the execution
Of well laid plans and conspiracies
So cruel and yet so beautiful

The kiss of the infinite falls upon you
Maybe once in a lifetime
When stars are uncrossed and wise words echo
You recognize the madman in yourself

V

I look forward to other ways of dying
Ways that won't affect the internal weather
But now it is too late
We will commit that sin again
Making the same damn mistake
Only this time it will cut much deeper

VI

Straight toward the maddening waters
We descend into the clay
And disappear
In a thundering range
To reach for our own decay

Spirits burn in the distance
Calling down the debris of generations
Searching for forever
Afraid of rising
Like a river's edge to nowhere

Borrowing light from grief
We honor our relations
The arch of your words
Will never cease
To inspire revolt in the herd

A spark goes off in the barren
The desert creates itself with a word
Where fear is king
Mouths are spiteful
And we choke on the smoke of lepers

VII

What language is this?
The glorious din of particles
Born of the dust and fire from other suns
Who now speak in muted tones
Of uselessness and transparency
In this age of eclipse
Of how the acceleration will devour us all
What language is this?

VIII

This is not a world
Where words are forgotten
Nor is this a world
In which I will be forgiven
Yet I trudge on and break trail
Like a goddamned bull
Solace doesn't lie with the civilized

IX

Mercurial by nature
The seeker is never satisfied
When we learn how to see the ritual architecture
We will know how to ask
If the sea is, in fact, deep enough
To hold all we would burden her with

X

The bleeding didn't help
The serum still foul
Jaws tight, faces grim
Preparing to receive the roaring waters

Gnostic repetition on goatskin
Singing the spirit disconnect
This land is holy and the truth is vast
Yet we have desecrated and defiled our temple

XI

The one-eyed man of the ocean
Lies in a state of disease
And in desperation
Seeks to kill the man with the sun
Yet only the vows of nature
Can dislodge the infected nights
From the misanthropic

XII

It's so damn easy
To justify the horrors done in your name
When your soul has already been conquered
And you identify most
With those who have conquered it

XIII

A tenuous hold at best
Reaching for the source
The source of breath
There in that wilderness
As it now remains nowhere
Where nothing yet exists
Save the solemn distances between us

XIV

The sun's daughter is singing
Singing to the sinking bodies
Driven to their own drawing down
Under the current, drowning

Tangled in driftwood barricades
Their feet blistered and black
From their failed and desperate attempt
To escape their burning lands

XV

Inscribed on bark, nailed to bone
The words were spoken
And thus repeated

Bind the false
Bind the lies
Bind disintegrating disease

Bring the true and I will release the sun
Bring truth and I will revel in the word
Bring us health and I will reveal humanity

Let no cunning witchery
Nor malicious treachery
Undo this good galdr

XVI

Dream states and earthworks
Weave the memory cloth
Synapses fire wildly
Imprint my brain with longing
For iron-age rites
And megalithic monuments

Geomantic structures
Irradiated by cyclical suns
Altar luminations of earthly things
Here is where the mind finds alignment
Here is where the soul finds release

XVII

Bleed the stars of their righteousness
Damn their condescending gaze
As if anything has ever come of ice

What are we really?
But the stories we tell ourselves
Carbon forged in dying stars
Taking a temporary shape
To dream, to struggle, to disappear

XVIII

The universe is never still
The sea is never quiet
The mind a burning furnace
Warped with fiery thought

The struggle gives meaning
To the otherwise mundane
Time, a triumphant terror
Its flower roots from injury

Unafraid we must heed the signs
Blissful in the attempt to overcome
What cannot be overcome
Dwelling in the heart of the infinite

Suffering the lonely
Amongst the multitude
Redeemed in the negative space
From which all has arisen

Bound by endless chain reaction

XIX

A furious alchemy it is…these words
Though often logical enough
The consequences remain clear

I am not speaking of cryptic parchments
Or barely discernible manuscripts
But of language itself

It simultaneously liberates and betrays
Preserves and destroys
Heals and infects
All the while placing us all in harm's way
In constant danger…of misunderstanding

XX

That which we adore is so incredibly fragile
As we cling to some sense of cosmic order
Only for a brief moment are we ever stable

Then fall back to our fractured nature
Is there any such thing as rest in our universe?
I will not fall prey to the spirit of the age

I will dive deep into the oldest waters
Where the light is so ancient
That it taught songs to the gods

XXI

This shroud does not become you
Your well is of despair
Despite my thirst, I will not drink here
Your dying star is wearisome

A hallucinatory psychology
Suspends doubt and common roles
Walk with the apparition across the threshold
Chant the wordless songs

Breathe in the storm
Its pattern is well known to you
Spit out the venom
It is what you meant to say anyway

A remarkable fragment of yourself
Descends upon the song of songs

XXII

Ignoring the watchful eye of our star
The frost burns its way across the earth's breast
Beware the messenger half buried in stone
Shield ourselves with skin
That our spirits do not drain
Or lie trapped beneath our souls
Which are not prepared for the mother
All shall hear her words in the end
Entranced and transfixed in our own transformation
Reshaping our realities into natural phenomena
This is not our first winter

XXIII

Damnation awaits these hours with silent waves
We are only visitors here borrowing wasted time
Cultivating an age of the grotesque

We circumnavigate the falls as lightning
Strikes the wonder and transcends watched omens
With the fierce radiance of a proud horse

Iron and rust run through the coals to quench in oil
With a consuming hunger to rise when fires flare
Inhabiting the imminent need of nature itself

AS THE CROW FLIES

1999

Stained Glass

The reflection of stained glass colors your face.
The light of day echoes your skin,
Giving summer's beauty the rightness of warmth.
These words in your mouth
Bring the sadness of a thousand winters.

Confusion builds a fire.
The smoke must clear to see and breathe.

The magic contained in the braiding of your hair.
A spirit entwined in a ritual knowing.
A gift, a token of the unexplained.
A grief that haunts me
To the ends of my mind.

Confusion builds a fire.
The smoke must clear to see and breathe.

We All Fall

When the golden bough breaks
The cradle of civilization
When our island sinks in the sea
Songs of the siren will lure us down

Ashes, ashes, we all fall

When the king is dead
And we ride wild horses
When we climb to the top of the mountain
And come tumbling down

Ashes, ashes, we all fall
Down

Remember

Dream through the seasons
Only to remember
Past becomes of the future
When all is said and done

Your life awaits you

Warning of a Storm

Staring out the window pane
Seeing through yourself
Counting your blessings again
Wondering when it will be
And how it will be then
See the warnings of a storm
As patterns unfold themselves
To try and be whole

Is this too much to ask
To live free with a quiet mind
And trust in someone else
I want to believe in the sun
Who in all its splendor is dying
I desire the solidness of earth
This ground is still shaking apart
What will be, will be

Twice Born

The wind sings alone for the martyr,
A man against the age.
Many called but few are chosen,
Twice born into the gaze.

Challenging man-made illusion,
The truth against the world.
Men go to graves with their truth,
Still the sun will rise.

Surrender mind to the mystery,
The seen and the unseen.
Sever head from their disgrace,
Religions founded and undone.

Midheaven

Why can't I rest a while? This unease in my chest.
A nauseous burning keeps me awake to swim inside.
To consume myself with fears of what I've given.
A piece of my breath, and the power to destroy.

In this house midheaven, my hopes and dreams are tied.
The archer's bow is lifted and takes aim at my heart.
Never did I catch sight of the weapon raised.
Though it had been woven into my weave of fate.

Shadows in Stone

Dawn of mists and mourning
Veil of ancient tears.
Near a tree lies a shallow grave.
Bones of earth grasping hands
With the roots of the past.
Fasting spirits to the land.

Chasing shadows in stones.
Clouds clear revealing
Awareness of the light.
Seeking forgotten longings,
Withered pathways to the wise.
From a peak I gaze the glory.

IF I SHOULD FALL TO THE FIELD

2002

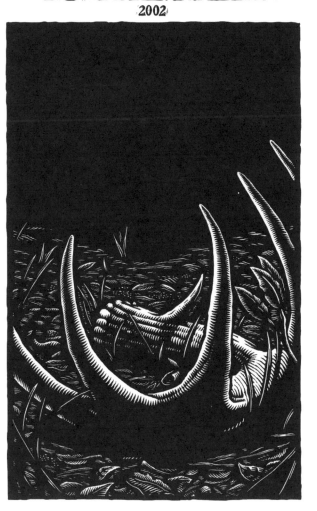

Breathe

You don't believe what you don't see,
Each grain of sand beneath the sea.
You have no faith in a dream,
Fade into the landscape unseen.
In a field of weeds, killing time,
A winding river rushes by.
All the while you seem to be going blind,
A cold numb grey in your eyes.

Breathe in, breathe deep.
A lifetime is too long to sleep.
Staring at lightning won't keep you warm.
You hear the thunder, but can't get out of the storm.

Growing weak and thin,
This has to end where it begins.
Waiting for winter's first snow,
To cover your tracks so no one will know.
That you ever lived, or ever lied,
You wouldn't give and never tried.
No words worth air ever sound,
From a flightless bird, bound to the ground.

Breathe in, breathe deep.
A lifetime is too long to sleep.
Staring at lightning won't keep you warm.
You hear the thunder, but can't get out of the storm.

To the Field

The winds outside are change.
Shadows move through the floor, chasing the light.
When the leaves fall to the field,
I'll know the wrong from yesterday.
Sky turns sustaining night.
We all watch the frost from the withered vines.
Of the autumn host I'll pray.
On my sustaining life,
I will be as yew, with the grain.

Driven through a sea,
The tides wash in to inspire.
The dawning moon of the mind,
Flesh gives way to the worlds in her eyes.
The rain will no longer cease,
Drowning gives meaning to breath.
I come down to stake my claim,
Runes in the clouds and blood on the bone.

Hallowed Ground

I stand exposed in a barren field
Like a stone bled dry
The daystar fades and darkness cools
The fever breaks, my sight is clear
A figure forms of shining gold
A guiding light that leads me
To a tree of reckoning
Where visions bring our name

Lie on, lie on hallowed ground

A stone carved face, an idol's stare
Calls us to the river
Ghosts of the past speak of things
We don't care to hear now
The sun bleached planks of this old wall
Meet the dust and cry out
Grandfather's hands bled for us here
Hallowed ground forever

Bleed on, bleed on hallowed ground

This River

This river runs to the South,
Like these thoughts flow from my veins.
Blood like fuel is fed to the fire,
Inspired by faces in the flames.

In a boat we crossed over the water,
The edge of the earth fell away.
On the banks we stood alone,
As dreams were washed out to sea.

The Wild Hunt

There's a candle in the window of the old thatch house.
Mother said it was a beacon on this night of the hunt.
She sang softly of those who were gone
As she poured whiskey on the stone near the hearth.

Howlin' beasts and unearthly cries,
A one-eyed rider storms the skies.

The windows started to shudder under the force of the wind.
Whirling mists became furies, rolling clouds became wolves.

Howlin' beasts and unearthly cries,
A one-eyed rider storms the skies.

Though I was young that night, never once did I fear.
I knew this ancestral spectre was a wandering god.
Known to our people forever, giver of breath and life.
I will gladly ride with him when it becomes my time.

Howlin' beasts and unearthly cries,
A one-eyed rider storms the skies.

Dawn

Under a blood red moon that fades from my eyes
An ancestral haunting brings their names across a plain
Unknown

Harvesting thought from a mind out of time
The disembodied voices of corpses on the wind
Unknown

A GRAVE IS A GRIM HORSE

2008

A Grave is a Grim Horse

You cut your eyeteeth on stone
Your feet stood firm in the soil
Your life is survived by your deeds
We will remember and honor your name

A grave is a grim horse to ride

I'll pass through the darkness this night
With my face pressed into the earth
Thin is the veil, thick is the skin
To cross the borderlands of flesh

A grave is a grim horse to ride

As I lie on this house of bones
Speak to me now of time's strange pass
Do ages repeat all the same?
Tell me what you see out there

A grave is a grim horse to ride

To cross this bridge of shadow
Visions of silence all told
What the dead reveal to the living
My blanket can't keep out this cold

A grave is a grim horse to ride

The Acre

Like an autumn wind, a chill on the bone
A shadow drags night across the sky
To see in the gut what is blind to the eyes
Seek counsel in the angle of the rain

You must work with the acre you are given
And read the signs of your days

Barren signs favor no plow
To all life's work there is a season
The water at your feet and the rich black earth
And the fire in your head

You must work with the acre you are given
And read the signs of your days

When the last golden shank hangs down
Like the old horns of the moon
If it rains on the long blasting days
The killing frost will bite down hard

You must work with the acre you are given
And read the signs of your days

Valley of the Moon

The vultures are flying lower than they used to.
They don't waste their time on old bleached bones.
It's too damn hot and I feel choked out.
Our past betrayed by smoke and mirrors.
All she gives is a stone façade,
Like ill given flowers at a dead man's wake.
Here, we slave for the dreams of another,
And fight over scraps like wayward dogs.

The ash under a red stone guides the way.
The embers of his words ignite our souls.
My love and I, we will follow.
We'll find our valley of the moon.

These words a mirror of his own heart
And the land he gave it to.
Looking back to the strength of our blood,
A great river of fortune and will.
All they gave, they gave for us,
A better life in a better land.

The ash under a red stone guides the way.
The embers of his words ignite our souls.
My love and I, we will follow.
We'll find our valley of the moon.

A place where we can be who we are,
And just what we were meant to be.
Plain to hold and see of what we're made:
Spirit, sinew, blood, and soil.

Up horses now! And straight and true
Let ever broken furrow run
The strength you sweat shall blossom yet
In golden glory to the sun[1]

The ash under a red stone guides the way.
The embers of his words ignite our souls.
My love and I, we will follow.
We'll find our valley of the moon.

[1] London, Jack, *The Valley of the Moon*, Mills & Boon, 1913.

Looking for Dry Land

A lonely man on the mountain
Looks down at what he sees
All those who lie beneath him
And the station of his peak
He cannot bear the weight
Of being so high
An island unto himself
Where clouds obscure the sky

Looking for dry
Looking for dry land
Waiting for his ship to come in

A worried man at the river
Stares across to the other side
To the risks he won't afford
And the failures he can't hide
The levee can't hold back the flood
The banks start to breach
He surrenders himself to the flow
While the crossing lies just out of reach

Looking for dry
Looking for dry land
Waiting for his ship to come in

A broken man in the ocean,
Drawn in by its sound
Clinging to the shallows,
Afraid of going down
Sings a shanty of his life
In a dialect now gone
His compass points away from himself,
The constellations move on

Looking for dry
Looking for dry land
Waiting for his ship to come in

Western Son

When all my days are done
And the western sea sets the sun
When all is said and done
I am a western son

I grow so tired of these little white lies
Kicking a proud dog with the weight of its kind
I've seen this rootless wander become the end of the line
You know it's a strange breed that volunteers its demise

When all my days are done
And the western sea sets the sun
When all is said and done
I am a western son

I've seen many a good man give their hearts to the east
Turn their thoughts, then damn the milk
From their own mother's breast
The grain withers on the stalk as they curse the strain
Darkness will close in on any seed that remains

When all my days are done
And the western sea sets the sun
When all is said and done
I am a western son

Brigit's Cross

Holy man, don't waste your breath on me,
I don't seek what you lost.
We don't need your superstition.

Keep your poison out of our well,
It's bitter to the taste.
We've been drinking here for thousands of years.

I left my blessing...on the Brigit's Cross

Our old ways are as snakes,
They live deep in the clay.
No man with a crooked stick can drive them away.

He drove our gods into the sea,
At least so they say.
Let me tell you friend, we've given up your ghost.

I left my blessing...on the Brigit's Cross

I live my days by the quartered wheel,
Woven from the straw.
Harvest gold reflects the sun.

I left my blessing...on the Brigit's Cross

A LIFE UNTO ITSELF

2015

In Your Wings

Coyotes call in a dark wood
I could have sworn they called my name
Their cries bring one to knowing
That either way it's all the same, all the same

Tracks lead me to the water
Moving glass stares right through me
Sundogs feed on a black moon
Their throbbing sound in my stomach, in my gut

All my life, all I've known
The raven's call has always shown
In your wings, in your light
In your dark all is right

If I had eyes to see myself
As you see me
A mouth full of curses
And a head full of fire, that never tires

Heather mounds will shelter me
The horse's heads will look away
The green king three times asks me
What is it you are seeking?
My way home.
My way home.

A Life Unto Itself

I will leave part of myself
On the backside of the mountain
Where the autumn winds blow right through me
And open my bones of highways and rivers

In the wake of this revelation
A wilderness of ways torn by thorns
In the unceasing rain and the harrow's final turn
I lower my head stricken by the awe of it all

Bury me in some ancient way
That my life might be worth a few words
Carved in stone for my kin
For to guide them as I have been

Though I've been this way before
I've completely lost my bearings
When will I ever learn to trust my own direction
When I have lost my way she always finds me

A life unto itself is hard to see
And not get swept away by waves of darkness
To stand tall and true to oneself
And the deepest part of your being

Bury me in some ancient way
That my life might be worth a few words
Carved in stone for my kin
For to guide them as I have been

A Language of Blood

Wires get crossed, sparks will fly
And this disillusion, a language of blood
Discontent speaks in voices
Reptilian mind survives at any cost

When the earth falls from under your feet
No sense of direction to lead you home
A drift of swans where two rivers meet
Fears leave your vision, tributes carry you

A thief in the light steals silver
A thief in the night steals fire
But the thief that hides inside you steals it all

If I could know just one thing, I'd know where I'm goin'
If I fear just one thing, I fear my own mind
If I could kill just one thing, I'd murder my self torture
If I could be just one thing, I'd be a stone on a hillside
If I could love just one thing, I would love love itself
If I could feel just one thing, I feel it in your body
If I believe just one thing, please believe in it with me
And we'll tell it to the stars

Birch Bark Box

This evening whispers a longing prayer
The lotus unfolding, the smell your hair
Wounds sealed with honey, now fading scars
Carry the promise of the stars

And the darkness in-between
From where all the answers lie
The farther I'm from fall away
To the fair one who waits

Cast the amber back to the sea
With all that I am and hope to be
The gifts you have given, so pure and true
See inside me as I reach inside you

Place the silence where it belongs
In that old birch bark box
The farther I'm from fall away
To the fair one who waits

The virtues spoken by tattered leaves
Skin the horses, blood returns to me
Oceans before us upholding the moon
Revealing the pattern amongst the stars

Chasing Ghosts

See down into this darkened draw
All that has been dredged from the lake
We'll shed no tears while chasing ghosts
The sea will feast upon the land

Eyes of my youth saw silver suns
I scratched my plans out in the sand
And dashed them all out on the stones
Too blind to see the road before me

I get so turned around inside
Words always fail to speak my mind
Madness cooled now by the fire
Sometimes I just can't shake the sick

Known But Not Named

Where all of my letters were written
In worlds and lifetimes now gone
Withered the sentiment, all but forgotten
As the great wheel rattles on

Symbols I carve with my knife in the hide
Reddened and sung
Words that are carried as gifts to the sky
Words in our tongue

Burdens I carry have preyed all along
My being denied of its peace
In need I sang the High One's first song
It all came to be

I stood in the river, in its powerful voice
And listened intent as it spoke
Of saner ways to walk in the world
Free from the weight of the yoke

A thought crept in my troubled mind
As my ship was sinking
To do as I had been done by
Of vengeance I was thinking
Tunnel vision, reddened sky
To twist their lives, see them suffer
Consumed by the weight of fire
My only dreams of blood

A white haired stranger wandered by
To warm his bones by the fire
He listened to my bloodstained plans
He did not judge or scorn
But shared the tales of his many lives
From both ends of the dagger
The actions that had dragged him down
And the path that set him free

His words were wise and I realized
My life had not been my own
Since I gave the reigns to fear and pain
And traded joy for madness
I saw the freedom he now had
And wanted it for my own
To swim the stream as it was
And leave my grief behind me

NO WILDERNESS DEEP ENOUGH

2020

Indifferent Eyes

I'll wake with the stars
I'll wake with the stars
Reach for the infinite deep
Free of the insanity

Scars never bled
Mirror my heart
Words never said
Mirror my soul
My soul
Mirror my soul
Again

Soon I'll be lighting the fire
For this untouchable place
Where spirit
Spirit has now taken flight
And the emptiness
The emptiness swallows us all

The wilderness inside our minds
Is Lost
To the sheltering sight of the blind
Indifferent eyes
This age of indifferent eyes
Is bleeding
Bleeding all over our lives

Reach for the infinite deep
The wilderness inside our minds
The emptiness swallows us all
Bleeding all over our lives

Reach for the infinite deep
The wilderness inside our minds
The sheltering sight of the blind
Is bleeding all over our lives
Bleeding all over our lives

The Old Straight Track

Nowhere to go
And nothing to say
We've burned the way
We've learned the lay
The ley of the lines
You lay it on the line

From where blood is letting
The finite rays of our light
We have the sea
We have the sea
And we'll always have the sky
And we'll always have the sky

Dreams of Trees

It often seems to be
Clearest at the stream
Dragged from the ocean and given eyes
Called from the wind as if we were wise

Still now you voices, let us rest
Carve the ash like a man possessed
When the weather changes your course
Bare to the heavens exposed

Shadows on the Run

If you want to save us from
The house that is burning down
Lead us through the flame
Remember all our names

The soul is what is left
When the spirit dies
The past will not erase
An undying embrace

The spiraling away
And months of blood ahead
Like shadows on the run
We've summoned what is done

Searching high and low
For something to behold
With reverence and grace
Before its time to fade

Call it what you will
The deadliest of all
Takes all that we adore
And everything we've known

Wild Iron

The firelight is burning low
The halfmoon sits behind us
Endless the days of unbroken plains
A ring of stars wild with iron

Giving ground back to the river
Trees gone bare of winter bones
Of the twelve, are we the aether
The all seeing eye has no way of knowing

Tear out my entrails to decipher
Wounded dream, fragile and phantom
Nightshade high country, oscillations
Motionless yet manifest

The silent stories we tell ourselves
Map the terrain of our true nature
A messenger of beasts and monsters
The source of the masks we wear

Trail the Silent Hours

The weight as evening comes
Let nothing go ungiven, nothing at all
These miscarried moments are all mine
Confusion carries us through the night
We will always stumble in the dark
And trail the silent hours tearing apart
We would not hear words given voice
But tore apart your altar to the void
Stand then as an oak, holding ground
Seek shelter in surrender, but don't give in

Acknowledgments:

I would like to give special thanks and maximum love to my soulmate, Niela Von Till. Your endless support and encouragement means the world to me. Emma and Freya, you are the most kind, beautiful, and intelligent daughters a man can ask for. I give thanks to my parents for the gift of life itself and always being supportive of my endeavors. Mazatl, the amazing artwork and meaningful conversations about life, spirit and art have been an absolute honor. Thomas Hooper and Jacob Bannon, I value greatly your friendship, inspiration, and advice. Josh Graham, thank you for your help and skills with the vector, video images, advice, and putting an extra set of eyes on my layout. Lucas Hutson, thanks for the constructive criticism and helpful opinions. And to duncan barlow, I greatly appreciate you being willing to take a chance on me and helping my vision become a reality.

Photo by James Rexroad

About the Author

Steve Von Till is an American musician, songwriter, educator, and poet. He is best known as a singer and guitarist in the highly influential and genre defying collective, Neurosis, which has been credited with changing the face of heavy music over the last 35 years. Since 1999 Von Till has composed and recorded five solo albums of his unique style of haunting Americana, the lyrics of which are contained in this volume. Under the guise of his alter ego, Harvestman, Von Till has recorded several rural psych albums including the film score for the Italian thriller, H2Odio. He oversees the fiercely independent record label, Neurot Recordings, from a pole barn outside his home in the forests of North Idaho where he also teaches elementary school. *Harvestman* is his first book of published poetry.